PC HARDWARE
EXPLAINED

WARNING

Contains explicit photos of hot computer hardware

V. Subhash

PC HARDWARE EXPLAINED

Written, illustrated & designed by

V. Subhash

First edition

Published in 2021 by V. Subhash
(www.VSubhash.in)

ISBN

For paperback: 978-93-5457-183-1

Acknowledgements

- Open-source fonts: Lato, Enterprise, Archivo Narrow and Budmo Jiggler
- Stock photos: Pixabay.com and Unsplash.com
- Other photo credits: Asus, BenQ, CoolerMaster, Crucial, EVGA, Intel and Western Digital

Table Of Contents

Introduction

I got my first personal computer (PC) in the year 2000. A couple of friends built it for me. It took us all day to buy the parts but assembling the computer took less than half an hour. Since then, I have built several desktop PCs, both for myself and for others. Just by watching my friends that day, I had picked up the skill of assembling PCs. It is that simple. Only equipment that anyone needs to build a desktop PC is a screwdriver set!

This is a testament to the *modular design* principle used to make personal computers (PCs). Just buy the parts and put them to together yourself, just as good as any store-bought branded PC. In fact, when you assemble a PC yourself, you can include more powerful parts for less money.

There is a catch to all this, right? Yes, it is true. Prior to buying the parts for my first PC, I had spent considerable time reading magazines like *PC Quest* and *CHIP* and hardware enthusiast sites like *AnandTech.com*. It took a lot of research before I finalized the parts. So confident was I that, unlike most people, I did not buy an Intel processor. Even in those years, I was sufficiently aware of the chip's giant's underhand tactics to squeeze out competitors and shake down the consumer.

When I learned HTML and created a website, my first article was titled *'PC Hardware Explained'*. All the knowledge that helped me build my first computer went into that article. It was the only article of its kind on the Internet for several years. PC hardware has evolved quite rapidly in the intervening 20-plus years and the article had become hopelessly obsolete.

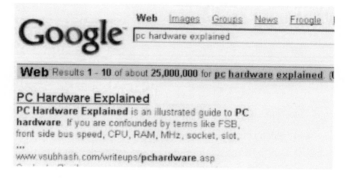

In 2020-21, I had become an author of over two dozen mostly non-fiction books. I felt that an updated version of the article would be welcome as a book. Despite laptop sales in the lead, people are still buying a lot of desktop PCs. This new and updated **PC Hardware Explained** has almost everything that a new buyer of a laptop or a builder of a desktop needs to know.

V. Subhash
26 December 2021
www.VSubhash.in

Scope

Most desktop and laptop PCs sold today use CPU chips made by Intel, AMD, or Apple.

Apple PCs or Macs are based on a closed proprietary system. Apple supplies both hardware and software. It is not possible to buy the parts from third-party suppliers and build a Mac. So, this book will just ignore that segment of the market.

There are some PCs that use ARM-licensed CPUs. These low-power CPUs are typically used in mobile phones and tablets. Google Chromebooks and Microsoft Surface are examples of such PCs. This book will ignore them too, as they do not provide much in terms of consumer choice. You can however build lightweight Internet-enabled computers with ARM-based chips such as the Raspberry PI. [7]

This book will concern itself with PCs that are based on Intel or Intel-compatible CPUs. There is only one other company that makes Intel-compatible CPUs and that is AMD. Intel used to dominate the CPU market but AMD has been making better CPUs than Intel for a long time. AMD had made such tremendous advances in CPU technology that Intel had had to license AMD's technology in its own CPUs.

Intel/AMD CPUs are supported on Windows and Linux operating systems (OSs). Both support a wide range of third-party hardware computer components. Intel/AMD CPUs and the Windows/Linux are popular choices for computer system builders.

OS	Intel	AMD	Apple
Windows	Yes	Yes	No
Linux	Yes	Yes	No
Mac	No	No	Yes

- AMD started calling their CPUs as **APUs** or **Accelerated Processing Units** after they integrated the graphics chip (video card) functionality on the same die as the CPU. This happened after AMD acquired the graphics card maker ATI.
- Apple used Intel CPUs for some years. During this time, it also allowed Windows and Linux OSs to be installed on Macs alongside the Mac OS. In 2021, Apple switched to its own ARM-based CPUs known as **Apple silicon** (M1) for its Macs. The Windows OS built for Microsoft Surface computers can be made to run on these Macs with some additional software.

CPU

A personal computer is usually identified by a display screen or monitor, computer case, keyboard and mouse. However, the **CPU** or the **Central Processing Unit** is at the heart of the computer. Or rather, it is the brains of the computer. It provides the computing power required to run itself, other hardware components and the installed software. When building/selecting a new desktop, the CPU is the first part that you need to choose. At any given time, several CPUs over a wide performance range are available in the market. Naturally, the best performing CPUs are costlier and lesser performing CPUs are cheaper. PC hardware enthusiast sites such as AnandTech.com or computer magazines like *Digit* or *PC Magazine* regularly test CPUs against a variety of benchmarking software. The results will tell which of those CPUs you can afford or want.

CPU socket

A CPU requires an electronic circuit board known as the motherboard. [8] Your choice of motherboards will be limited to a certain type of *CPU socket* supported by your choice of the CPU. This is a big socket on the motherboard over which the CPU is installed. The CPU socket has several holes in which the pins on the underside of the CPU can be securely seated.

The CPU sockets for Intel CPUs are different from those for AMD CPUs. The shape and design of the CPUs will be different. This means that you cannot install an Intel CPU in a motherboard meant for an AMD CPU. Similarly, an AMD CPU cannot be used on an Intel CPU motherboard. Intel and AMD CPUs are only software-compatible, not motherboard-compatible.

Other computer components such as RAM modules [16] or add-on (expansion) cards [10] are compatible with both Intel and AMD CPUs, as they follow open industry standards.

Every few years, the CPU manufacturer will change the design of the CPU socket and the CPU to incorporate new technologies, and also to make improvements and fix problems in the existing design. This is referred as a new *generation* or *family* of CPUs. It is a set of CPUs that have the same compatibility list.

CPU Family	Manufacturer	Socket
Threadripper	AMD	TR4
Ryzen	AMD	AM4
Phenom II	AMD	AM3
Alder Lake	Intel	LGA 1700
Rocket Lake	Intel	LGA 1200

Within a *CPU family*, the constituent CPUs differ only in how well they perform. This would mean that motherboards built for an older CPU family will not be compatible with members of a newer CPU family, even though they are all from the same manufacturer.

You will have to go to the website of the CPU manufacturer and find out what kind of CPU socket it requires on the motherboard. The motherboard choice will in turn dictate how many video cards [19] and add-on cards you can use.

Clock speed

The number of computing operations that a CPU can make in a second used to be called as the *speed of the CPU*. It is measured in gigahertz or 1 billion operations per second. The more faster the clock speed, the more data it can process and more jobs it can finish. Most people try to buy the CPU with fastest clock speed their money can buy.

Multi-core CPUs

CPU clock speed is somewhat a misleading measure of CPU performance because most CPUs available in the market today are *multi-core CPUs*. These are multiple CPUs built into one package — each core is a functional CPU. AMD was first to create a multi-core CPU when they realized that they could not forever go on increasing the speed of their CPUs. In 2005, they released a CPU that had two computing units working together. (Intel seems to have got wind of this ahead of time. It glued together two CPUs and claimed 'here are your first dual-cores'.) As of writing this, the **AMD Threadripper Pro** CPU beats competition with 64 cores!

Intel introduced a technology called **HyperThreading**. It enabled a CPU to process instructions in two execution pipelines simultaneously. It had the effect of having two CPUs run in sync with each other. Today, CPUs have multiple cores and each core executes two threads. That 64-core *Threadripper* CPU mentioned earlier can run 128 threads!

Other 'specs' (technical specifications)

- **Memory Support**: A CPU supports only certain types of RAM modules, say, 'DDR4 RAM up to a speed of 3200 MHz'. The specs of Intel Alder Lake processors say its supports DDR4 and DDR5. You will understand over the next chapters that this cannot happen on the same motherboard.
- **Graphics core count & frequency**: An AMD processor usually integrates a graphics chip. This part of the CPU is also made up of computing cores. Like the CPU clock speed, the graphics core also operates at a frequency. The *AMD Ryzen 5 5600* CPU has 6 CPU cores and 7 graphics cores. The CPU cores can run at a maximum speed of 4.4 GHz while the graphics cores can run at a maximum speed of 1.9 GHz.
- **Lithography**: A CPU has millions of transistors. They are etched on a silicon die using a process known as *CPU lithography*. The die size has been steadily reduced and the number of transistors has increased thanks to improvement in lithography technology. In the year 2000, CPUs were made with 42nm transistors. Now, we have CPUs made with 7nm transistors. The 'nm' abbreviation stands for *nanometre* or one-billionth of a metre.
- **TDP: Thermal Design Power** is a measure of how much power that a CPU consumes is dissipated (wasted) as heat. It is specified in watts. CPU will not always run at its top clock speed. It may automatically throttle itself when the computer is idle or is handling light loads. The TDP can also be lowered using software.

Heatsink and fan

A CPU is usually sold with a stock heatsink and fan. The CPU gets hot when it is running. The heatsink is a chunk of finned aluminium that can attracts this heat away from the CPU. The fan just blows away the heat away from the heatsink. Some heatsink thermal compound is also sold with the CPU. You need apply this paste on the outer surface of the CPU where you place the heatsink. This will help better conduction of the CPU heat into the heatsink. The thermal compound may also be factory-applied to the heatsink.

A system on a board: Raspberry PI

Raspberry PI looks like a tiny motherboard but it has a built-in CPU and RAM. You just need to add an SD card with an operating system so that it can function like a regular desktop. Most users use it as a souped-up media player and streamer. It consumes very little power — just 5 volts. A phone charger or power bank can run it. It has an HDMI ports so that you can connect it to a TV like a DVD player. It has an ethernet LAN port and can connect to

your Internet modem or router. Most PI users put it in a plastic case and place it next to their computer or TV. If you have an old-style television, then you can use this device to convert it to a 'smart TV'. Just install the Kodi app for Raspberry PI.

Motherboard

Motherboard or mainboard is the main circuit board of the computer. It provides numerous sockets, slots, connectors and ports for other computer components to be connected to it. This includes the CPU, RAM modules (memory sticks), storage discs, input devices (keyboard and mouse), add-on cards and the power supply (SMPS). When you turn on the computer, it is the motherboard that gets switched on first. A chip on the motherboard known as BIOS checks the motherboard, CPU, RAM modules and other installed devices. It displays the results on the screen and then hands over control to the CPU. The CPU then runs the computer. This startup sequence is known as the BIOS POST (Power-On Self-Test).

When you buy the motherboard, you need to ensure that the motherboards supports the CPU you are buying. The CPU manufacturer's website will guide you on this. Tech news websites and magazines will also do the same. After selecting the motherboard, the next thing you need to select is the memory modules [16] but more on that later.

Form factor

Motherboards are all rectangular in shape but they are built in a set of standard sizes known as *form factors*. ATX is the most popular form factor.

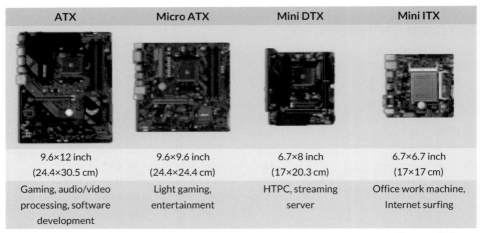

ATX	Micro ATX	Mini DTX	Mini ITX
9.6×12 inch (24.4×30.5 cm)	9.6×9.6 inch (24.4×24.4 cm)	6.7×8 inch (17×20.3 cm)	6.7×6.7 inch (17×17 cm)
Gaming, audio/video processing, software development	Light gaming, entertainment	HTPC, streaming server	Office work machine, Internet surfing

Photo credit: Asus

With an ATX motherboard, PC components do not get cramped and there is lot more room for air to flow. They also provide maximum expandability by providing extra ports and slots for connecting other components. The beige-coloured computer case that everyone is familiar with is called an ATX case because it accommodates an ATX-size motherboard. Sometimes, expandability and extra features provided by the ATX form factor is of less importance. For someone building a home-theatre PC (HTPC), a mini-ITX motherboard would do. For someone cramped for space, a mini-ITX motherboard might be a good choice, as its case can be bolted to the back of the display.

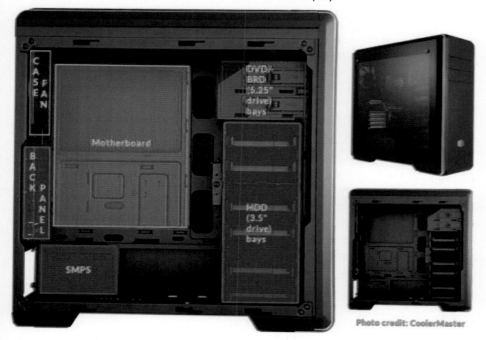

Photo credit: CoolerMaster

Extra features

For mainstream CPUs (middle-of-the-road ones in terms of performance), motherboard makers usually provide one or two cheap motherboards. More expensive models will have more features. Some of the fancier features are dual or quad GPU (video card) support, M.2 slots, integrated graphics, onboard audio, overclocking, heatsinks, watercooling support, dual LAN ports (10 or 2.5 gigabit), RGB headers (for lighting RGB 5050 LED strips), BIOS backup, and additional USB ports.

Power supply (SMPS)

External mains power cord

24-pin ATX connector for motherboard

6+2-pin PCIe connector to video card

4+4 pin EPS connector to MB for CPU

Power connector to SATA drives

4-pin Molex power connector for old/peripheral devices

Photo credit: EVGA

The motherboard and the CPU works on direct current (DC). The DC is supplied from a box inside the computer case known as the **SMPS (Switch-Mode Power Supply)**. The

SMPS is connected to the electrical mains (alternating current or AC) with a power cord. The power switch on the back of the PC is part of the SMPS, as does the socket which the power cord uses to plug into the computer. The computer fan noise that you hear is mostly from the fan inside the SMPS. The SMPS is not part of the motherboard but an important part of the PC. Inside the computer case, the ATX will have numerous cables and connectors to supply DC power to various components such as the motherboard, video card, disc drives, add-on cards and fans.

Chipset

Current CPUs have direct access and control of the RAM and video card.

CPU Family	Manufacturer	Socket	Chipset	Memory
Threadripper	AMD	TR4	TR4, sWRX8	DDR4
Ryzen	AMD	AM4	A520, B550	DDR4
Phenom II	AMD	AM3+	990X	DDR4
Alder Lake	Intel	LGA 1700	Z690	DDR5,DDR4
Rocket Lake	Intel	LGA 1200	Z490	DDR4

Access to other PC components such as disc drives, USB ports, onboard audio, networking and add-on (expansion) cards is performed through an intermediate chip on the motherboard known as the chipset. When a CPU manufacturer introduces a new CPU socket, it also releases new chipsets for motherboard makers to use.

PCI Express

When *PC Hardware Explained* was first written over 20 years ago, motherboards did not have so many features. They simply connected the disc drives to the CPU. Even graphics subsystem was provided using an 'add-on' video card. If you wanted audio, you bought a sound card. If you wanted to connect to the LAN, you bought a LAN card. The add-on card was inserted into a **PCI (Peripheral Component Interconnect)** slot. PCI slots were placed on the motherboard near back of the computer case so that external cables or equipment could be connected to the backplates of the add-on cards. My favourite PCI add-on card was a TV tuner card. It allowed me to record cable TV on my computer.

The slow error-prone PCI technology was later replaced with **PCI Express (PCIe)**.

Instead of dedicated data channels of the past, PCIe uses anything-goes pipelines known as PCIe lanes between the CPU and other components. These are faster and make optimum use of CPU cycles, data channels and power. Unlike PCI, which had a common slot design, PCIe slots come in several different profiles depending on how much power they might draw. A graphics PCIe card uses the widest x16 PCIe slot and have up to 16 PCIe lanes dedicated to it. The x1 slot (using one PCIe lane) is popular with manufacturers who create PCIe add-on (expansion) cards that provide backward compatibility to old devices (such as floppy drives and PATA hard disks) and forward compatibility for newer devices (such as mobile phones with USB C ports). Although the PCIe standard provides for x4 and x8 *slots* but they are not seen on any motherboard today. (However, there may be x4 and x8 *lanes* used between various components on the motherboard.) PCIe has undergone several generations of improvements. The transfer rate for x16 slot has improved from 4 GB per second in PCIe 1.0 to 63 GB per second in PCIe 5.0. PCIe versions are backward compatible.

SATA ports

These ports are used for connecting SATA hard disc drives (HDDs) [17] to the motherboard. (SATA stands for **Serial AT Attachment**. The **AT** has its origins in the IBM PC/AT of the 1980s.) A SATA hard disc has two ports — one for data and one for power. A **SATA cable** is used to connect the data port on the disc to a SATA port on the motherboard. The power connector from the SMPS is connected to the power port. (SATA HDDs are mounted on **drive bays** inside an ATX case.) SATA HDDs are available in form factors of 3.5 inches (for desktops) and 2.5 inches (for laptops).

USB ports

USB or **Universal Serial Bus** evolved as a standard for a high-speed daisy-chaining plug-and-play devices. The most popular implementation was much less glamorous, as a USB phone charger. Most other uses were of USB flash drives, USB card readers and USB modems. The standard has been through several revisions and USB 4 is the latest version. It has a lot of bandwidth and can simultaneously handle file transfers and video card output. Previous USB versions were plagued with multiple connectors. USB 4

Version	Speed	Symbol
USB 1	12 Megabit/sec	
USB 2	480 Megabit/sec	
USB 3 (USB 3.2 Gen 1)	5 Gigabits/sec	SS⟵⁵
USB 3.1 (USB 3.2 Gen 2x1)	10 Gigabits/sec	SS⟵¹⁰
USB 3.2 (USB 3.2 Gen 2x2)	20 Gigabits/sec	SS⟵²⁰
USB 4	40 Gigabits/sec	

has just one connector — USB Type C.

A few USB ports (coloured yellow or red) are powered by the motherboard even before the computer is started or even after the computer has been shutdown. Check the motherboard manual and connect their headers to the front-panel USB ports of your computer case.

M.2 slots

This slot is designed to accept an M.2 module. The most popular use for an M.2 module is as an SSD drive. It is a popular option on laptops and are usually identified as an **NVMe (Non-Volatile Memory Express)** drive. M.2 modules providing WiFi and Bluetooth functionality are also available. On one end of a M.2 module, there is a connector. On the other, there is an arch to accommodate a retention nut. There may be two to four retention holes on the motherboard to accommodate M.2 modules of different lengths.

NVMe SSD (M.2 module)

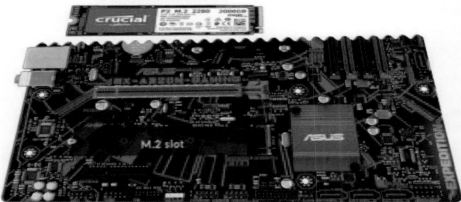

M.2 slot

Video card output ports

The computer screen or the display monitor is connected to a video card using a cable. The connector on either end has to be plugged in to one of these ports.

- **VGA (Video Graphics Array)**: This is an old standard that has been phased out.
- **DVI (Digital Visual Interface)**: This is also an old technology. This video output port exists on modern video cards so that people who have VGA displays can use a DVI-to-VGA converter.
- **DisplayPort**: This is the current video output standard.
- **HDMI (High-Definition Multimedia Interface)**: This port is used to output the computer screen to a TV or a projector with a HDMI cable. HDMI simultaneously transfers audio with the video.

Other ports

Motherboards pack so many features that the need for add-on (expansion) cards have been greatly diminished — so much so that the x1 PCIe slots on most motherboards remain unoccupied. The first motherboard has an IGP (integrated graphics processor) and it has video outputs for DisplayPort (to monitor) and HDMI (to TV) connections. It also has 4 USB 3.2 Gen 1 (Type A) ports, two USB 3.2 Gen 2x1 (Type A) ports, one USB 3.2 Gen 2x2 Type C port, one USB 3.2 Gen 2x1 Type C port, one 2.5 gigabit ethernet port (LAN), an optical audio out, and 8-channel audio. The audio jacks by default support 4.1 surround. If the line-in and microphone jacks can be re-configured as side and centre channels, then you can have 7.1 surround sound.

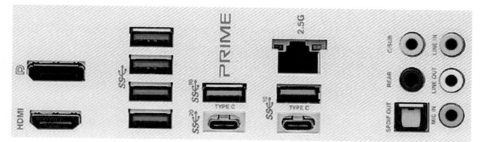

The second (gaming) motherboard requires discrete GPUs so there no video outputs on the backpanel. There is onboard WiFi (with two antenna mounts), two ethernet LAN ports (10 gigabit), 8 USB 3.2 Gen 2x1 (Type A) ports, two USB 3.2 Gen 2x2 (Type C) ports, an optical audio out, and 8-channel audio.

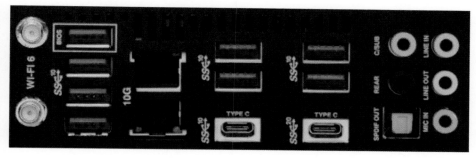

Misconfiguration

The motherboard has a clock (realtime clock or RTC) chip. It is powered by a button cell battery (known as the BIOS battery) even when the PC is powered off. That way, accurate time is maintained between use. When the battery runs out, the BIOS resets to a default older date. It may also lose any settings that you have changed in the 'BIOS Setup' program [21]. If you make mistakes with the motherboard settings and the computer becomes unbootable, you can reset the BIOS by removing the battery, shorting the terminals and putting battery back in again. In 'premium' (expensive) motherboards, there are backup chips for the BIOS and even a 'BIOS reset button'.

Motherboard layout

The layout of components on a motherboard varies across models. The names of the components will printed on the board but due to paucity of space the wording is often cryptic. Take the motherboard in your hands and study the layout. Compare what you see with the layout diagram printed in the motherboard manual. In the next two pages, a sample motherboard layout is available. You can practice identifying the components with it. Remember that it is just an illustration and your motherboard will have a different layout.

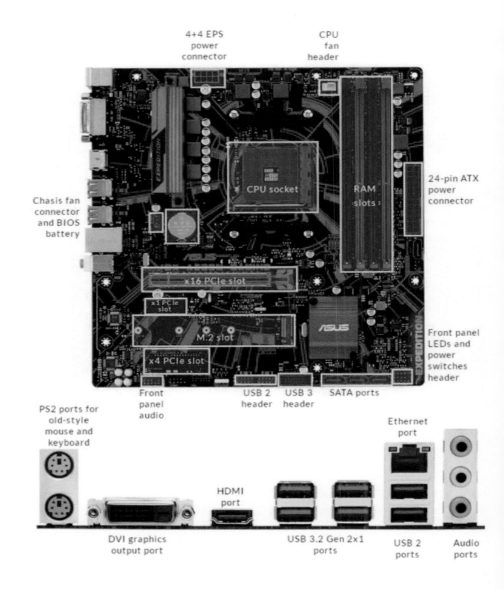

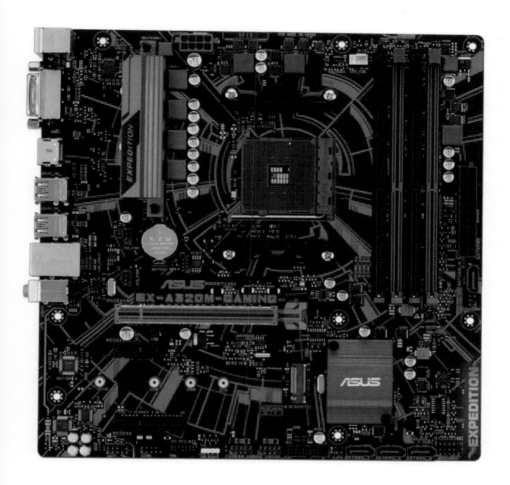

Memory and storage

In computer terminology, *memory* means a place to store data. The CPU has some fast memory on its die. They are called **L1, L2 and L3 caches.** The CPU can make very fast *reads* and *writes* to these caches. The cache memory is never enough so the CPU uses memory provided in RAM modules or memory sticks. This external memory is often referred as **system RAM**. This RAM holds data as long as the PC is powered on. (RAM is an abbreviation of *Random Access Memory*.)

RAM modules

The RAM type popular today is known as DDR4. DDR is an abbreviation of **Double Data Rate.** When it was introduced, it transfer data at double the rate of the older SD-RAM type. DDR has evolved to DDR5 now. In the popular **DDR naming convention**, the number of transfers per second (product of internal clock speed and number of bits prefetched) is mentioned after the DDR type. For example, DDR4 1600 performs 1600 transfers per second. As DDR use 8 bytes or 64 bits

Type	Bits	Clock speed	Bandwidth
DDR 200	2	100.0	1,600
DDR 400	2	200.0	3,200
DDR2 400	4	100.0	3,200
DDR2 1066	4	266.6	8,533
DDR3 800	8	100.0	6,400
DDR3 2133	8	266.6	17,066
DDR4 1600	8	200.0	12,800
DDR4 3200	8	400.0	25,600
DDR5 4800	16	300.0	38,400
DDR5 8400	16	525.0	67,200

per cycle, this translates to 12,800 million bytes per second or 1,02,400 bits per second. The industry naming convention uses the bandwidth value so DDR4 3200 is named as PC4 25600.

Of note is that, in DDR4, the bits prefetched per cycle did not increase to 16 but in DDR5 it has. The bandwidth is not the only improvement in each generation. Data density and operating voltages have also improved.

An advantage with DDR RAM is that you can use them in pairs and effectively double the memory bandwidth available to the CPU. For example, instead of using just one 32 GB RAM stick, buy two 16 GB RAM sticks. RAM slots may be coloured differently and spaced out in pairs so that you can enable **dual-channel configuration.** If you have two memory sticks of equal capacity, you can place one in each pair. If you use four sticks, then dual-channel configuration will be automatically enabled, as all slots are populated. Bear in mind that the memory bandwidth mentioned here are all theoretical limits. In real-world conditions, the bandwidth will likely to be limited by the slower performance of the CPU and the software, which may be acting as bottlenecks. Here is a fun idea: Create two temporary RAM drives in your OS and copy data among them to see if you can really reach the limits.

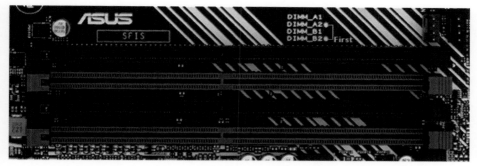

When you buy RAM modules, you need to buy those with the least **CAS latencies**. **Column Address Strobe** latencies are a measure of delays in fetching data from them. The lower the latency, the faster it performs. And, of course, more expensive. DDR4 RAM is available with latencies of CL 15 to CL 22. CL 22 memory will do fine for most tasks — the delays are in nanoseconds. Some extreme fellows such as gamers use CL 15 memory modules. These expensive memory modules also need heatsinks. It is a niche market so do not waste much time about it.

If your motherboard requires DDR4, then you have to use DDR4 RAM modules. You cannot use DDR, DDR3 or DDR2 in its place, as they are shaped differently. Desktop RAM sticks may be referred as **DIMM** and laptop RAM sticks may be referred as **SO-DIMM**.

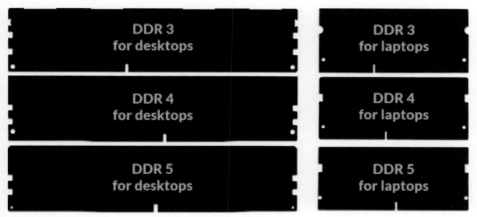

Hard disc drives (HDDs)

The other kind of memory on a computer is more permanent. It is available in the form of hard discs, optical discs (CD and DVDs) and USB storage drives. Data stored on these memories will last even after a power-down.

Hard discs are where you store your files. There are two types of them today — mechanical drives and solid state drives (SDD). Mechanical drives are an older technology but they offer more space for less money. They are less tolerant of shocks and vibrations as they have moving parts (magnetic discs (rotating at 5400 or 7200 rpm) and read-write heads). SDD drives have no moving parts and use erasable **flash memory** chips for storing data. They are more expensive but very robust and fast (faster than mechanical drives).

Hard discs come in several form factors. On laptops, **2.5-inch HDDs** are used. On desktops, **3.5-inch HDDs** are used. The mechanical drives come in both form factors. SDDs are only available in 2.5-inch HDD form factor. SDDs are also available in the form of M.2 modules. They are then known as NVMe drives [12]. USB disc drives with flash memory are also available. They are known by a variety of names *pen drives*, *thumb drives* and *USB flash drives*. Because they are so tiny, their capacities are comparatively limited.

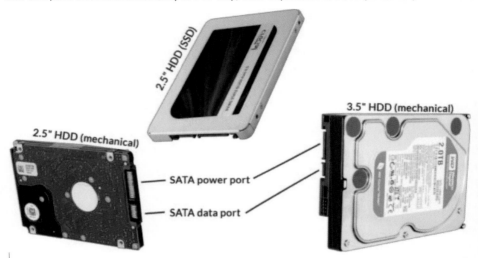

HDDs can be combined together in hardware and software to form **RAID (Redundant Array of Inexpensive Disks)** storage. There are several RAID configurations for achieving data striping and data mirroring goals. In the former, data is spread over multiple discs achieving faster operations. In data mirroring, data in some hard discs are mirrored in a redundant set of hard discs. A combination of both is also possible to recover from disc failures. RAID setups are somewhat complicated and not many people use them but the feature is available in a lot of motherboards.

Optical discs

DVD disc drives and Bluray disc drives are known as optical drives, as they use lasers and light sensors to read data etched on 'optical media'. With the easy availability of flash memory USB discs, the need for DVD drives has greatly diminished. It is still a convenient medium to buy movies. Bluray drives never really caught on with the public because they are very complex and expensive. Most optical media, such as movies and device driver discs, are read-only. You cannot write fresh data on them. Blank read-and-write DVD discs are also available. The process of writing data to them is known as 'burning'. It is a hassle and not many people bother with it any more.

Video Card

In early computers, the CPU handled the graphics display. Later, a dedicated video card was used to offload this task from the CPU. Today, a video card is also known as a **GPU** or **Graphics Processing Unit**. Like a CPU, the GPU comes with its own computing cores and high-speed graphics-optimized memory banks. They also have their own fans because they also run hot.

When a dedicated video card is used, it is known as a **discrete GPU**. On some motherboards, the video card functionality is integrated on the motherboard as a separate chip or as part of the CPU. Then, it is known as **integrated GPU**. An integrated GPU is not as powerful as a dedicated GPU but for simple tasks and light gaming and entertainment, it is more than enough. A discrete GPU is required only by gaming enthusiasts. Or, if the integrated GPU has some fault and you do not want to replace the whole rig.

As gaming became popular and multiple display screens became needed, support for simultaneously using multiple video card was added. AMD's solution is known as **CrossFire**. It's competitor nVidia's solution is known as **SLI (Scalable Link Interface)**. Intel does not have a dog in this game. Intel CPU motherboard manufacturers license CrossFire and SLI technologies for their multi-GPU motherboards. In multi-GPU configurations, the power draw is higher. Noise increases and additional cooling is required.

All motherboards will have at least one x16 PCIe slot. The video card will be inserted in this slot. You will have to provide additional power to it using the 6+2 pin connector(s) from the SMPS. On multi-GPU motherboards, two to seven x16 PCIe slot may be available. Unused PCIe lanes can be used to provide additional storage using a special x16 PCIe add-on card in an unoccupied x16 slot.

Gaming video card

Fan-less video card for HTPCs and light gaming

RAID add-on card that sits in a x16 PCIe slot and suports 4 NVMe SSDs.

Display

The computer screen or monitor is the TV-like device that most people associate with a computer. It occupies a lot of real estate but has limited computing ability. It is nothing more than a display or output device, just as keyboard and mouse function as input devices.

Today, LCD panels are used as computer displays both on desktops and laptops. There are three types of LCD panels. Each have their own advantages and disadvantages.

Feature	TN	VA	IPS
Response time	< 1ms	4-5ms	1-2ms
Color	Poor	Good	Best
Contrast	Good 1000:1	Best 3000:1	Good 1000:1
Viewing angle	170/160	178/178	178/178
Suitable content	Fast action	HDR	Visual richness

Source: BenQ

The response time (in milliseconds) refers to how quickly the screen pixels (the dots on the screen) can react to changes in the visual content. Color reproduction is dependent on the ability of the screen to display a wide variety of colours. Contrast ratio is the range between extremes of dark and lit content that the monitor can display. Compared to CRT (cathod-ray tube) monitors of yore, LCD panels support much less horizontal and vertical viewing angles. However, they are not slackers.

TN panels are fast and cheap. Their viewing angles are lesser than the other two types. They are inferior in color reproduction and contrast ratio. IPS panels are best in color reproduction but they are not suitable for HDR (High Dynamic Range) content.

(Think of HDR as several shades of dark.) What appears as dark regions in a VA panel may appear as black on an IPS panel. VA panels are all-rounders. They may be slower in gaming performance but they have the best combination of color reproduction and contrast ratio.

Other features that you need to check in a monitor are:

- Screen width — for multiple desktops and docked windows
- Aspect ratio — ratio of screen width and height
- Brightness — to eliminate glares caused by other light sources, not important if you sit close to the monitor all the time
- DisplayPort and HDMI ports — VGA and DVI are obsolete
- VESA bracket support — for mounting on a wall or attaching a Micro ITX [8] computer case

Some vanity features include:

- USB-C port — to send monitor output to a device that does not have regular video ports (a mobile phone for example)
- Brightness sensor
- Speakers
- Screen curvature

Laptop hardware considerations

When buying a new laptop, check these:

- **Screen width**: Big screens consume more battery power and small screens can make you squint. Use a small-screen laptop for travel. At home where you have more convenience, use a big-screen laptop.
- **Screen resolution**: If you are getting a new laptop, do not buy one with a 1336x768 screen resolution. Start with 1920x1080.
- **Thinness**: Almost all PC manufacturers try to imitate Apple and create very thin laptops. Their size limits air flow our inside the chassis and the touchpad can become hot. Their lack of heft prohibits any rough handling.
- **Battery life**: If you are the type that uses a laptop for several years, buy a spare battery. They are hard to acquire after the manufacturer moves on to newer models. Tip: Batteries need to be regularly used. If not, their *wear level* will increase and the store less charge.
- **NVMe slot**: This is a must-have feature as you can add a fast second hard disk.
- **Extra HDD bay**: If your laptop comes with an NVMe SSD disk, then its capacity may not be very large. If you are a software developer, gamer or a content creator, even a 1TB mechanical HDD is not enough and they put in a tiny 256 GB NVMe SSD disk! However, if the laptop has an empty extra HDD bay, you will be able to add a higher-capacity mechanical HDD and drastically increase the storage capacity of the laptop.
- **RAM upgradability**: If the laptop comes with an empty second RAM slot you can add an equivalent capacity RAM module and use it in dual-channel mode. If both slots are populated, then you will have to replace both modules with higher-capacity RAM modules.
- **Ethernet port**: Again, aping Apple, a lot of manufacturers have eliminated ethernet (wired LAN) ports. It is a stupid decision. Wireless LAN speeds cannot come close to wired LAN speeds. Wireless access is a drain on the laptop battery while wired LAN is powered by the router or the network switch. Besides, always-on wireless networks are inherently wasteful and a security risk. They greatly contribute to global warming and are probably a health hazard.
- **Keyboard usability**: Once again, aping Apple, manufacturers have reduced the size of keys. Their worst offence is the elimination of free space around the oft-used arrow keys.
- **USB C**: This is the most fastest port today and can provide a lot more voltage power several connected devices. It can also output video and network access to devices that do not have ports for them.
- **Operating system**: There is no need to pay extra premium for the Windows OS and/or Office productivity suite. Although not well advertised, laptops without the OS are available at a considerable discount. Just install Ubuntu Linux OS and LibreOffice. With Linux, you do not have to worry about installing drivers. Install the Mate desktop and say goodbye to annoying OSs.
- **UPS**: Even though there is a built-in battery, it is better to connect the laptop to the mains through an UPS. The UPS has a very good power filter and stabilizer. A lot of unexplained hardware failures can be eliminated if the AC power supply is clean.

How to assemble a PC

I would not recommend that you assemble a PC without having at least once watched someone else do it from start to finish. Highly edited online videos cannot count. At least for the first time, do it with the guidance of someone who knows how to assemble a PC. Without expert assistance, you might apply too much force or too little force and run into problems. No book is a substitute to real practical experience.

Precautions: Handle PC components with care. If a pin is bent or a solder joint becomes loose, the entire component will become unusable. Before starting, discharge your body of excess static electric energy by (grounding yourself by) touching a reasonably big metallic object such as a steel chair. Do not wear woollen clothes. You must not be dropping beads of sweat on the components so make the room comfortably airy but not too drafty. Remember that you cannot make connections too tight or too loose. Read all manuals. Installation procedure prescribed by them is more relevant than the following generic description of the steps.

- **Install CPU**: Stack some old newspapers and place the motherboard over it. Get the CPU and heatsink-fan combo out. Relax the CPU retention lever on the motherboard. Align the CPU properly and gently insert it into the socket. Snap back the retention lever. The thermal compound would have been already factory-applied to the heatsink. If it has a foil, remove it. Place the heatsink over the CPU and tighten the screws that came with it. Connect the CPU fan power cable to its header (pins) on the motherboard. DO NOT START THE PC WITHOUT THIS FAN POWER CONNECTION.

- **Install RAM**: Relax the retention snaps on both sides of the memory slots. Properly align the RAM modules and insert them into the slots. Knock the retention snaps on the modules.

- **Install motherboard**: Spread some more newspapers and place the computer case on them. Remove the left panel. Find the packet of screws, nuts and washers in the case and place it outside.

Find the plastic standoffs that came with the motherboard and insert them in the holes meant for them from the underside of the motherboard. They prevent the motherboard components coming into contact with the metallic side of the case.

Place the case on its right side. Screw in the metallic mounting standoff screws on the inside of the right side. Place the motherboard over them and secure it with screws.

- **Install the video card**: In the x16 PCIe slot, insert the video card. Remove the knockoffs on the back of the case so that the video ports can be accessed from the outside. Screw the back plate of the card to the case. Connect the video card fan(s) to the correct header on the graphics card if not already connected.

- **Install SMPS**: Slide the SMPS in its place in the case and screw it down. If there is a slider for voltage selection, set it for the kind in your country. (Do not power it yet.) Connect the (internal) 24-pin ATX connector from the SMPS to the motherboard. (Refer to the motherboard manual here.) Connect the 4+4 EPS connector (for the CPU) to the motherboard. Connect the 6+2-pin PCIe connector to the video card.

Connect the case fans to the 4-pin Molex connector.

- **Connect power headers**: The case has a few wires that need to be connected to the motherboard. They are for the power switch, restart switch, power LED, HDD activity LED and case speaker signal. (Refer to the manual and very carefully perform this step.) At this stage, the computer is ready to be tested.

Connect the AC power cord to the SMPS and switch on the power supply. The motherboard power LED on the motherboard should light up. The CPU fan should spin and then stop. If not, switch off power and remove the power cord from the mains and check everything. If the power LED does light up, switch off power and remove the cord from the mains.

Connect a display monitor to the video card. Connect its power cord to the mains. Switch on power to the SMPS again. Turn on the power switch on the computer case. The CPU fan will spin and the motherboard doing the POST test will be seen on the monitor. Otherwise, switch off power and remove the power cord from the mains and check everything. If the test went well and has finished, press the reset switch. The display should show the computer restarting. Listen for any beeps during startup. The motherboard manual will tell if you if they have a special meaning. If you hear anything, switch off power and remove the power cord from the mains and check everything.

- **Install drives**: Get the screws for mounting the drives. Slide the drives in their bays — DVD drives in 5.25" bays and HDDs in 3.5" bays. Before installing optical drives in the 5.25" bays, you will have to remove the front-side covers by relaxing the snaps on their sides from the inside. Connect the SATA power connectors [11] from the SMPS to the power ports of the drives. Connect the data ports to the SATA ports on the motherboard using SATA cables that came with the motherboard.

- **Install front panel devices**: Your computer case may have USB ports and audio connectors. Connect them to their internal headers on the motherboard. If your motherboard has USB headers that can provide power even when the computer is shutdown, connect them to the front panel USB ports, particularly if they are coloured yellow or red. If not, connect them free USB headers you find on the motherboard.

  Organize cables inside the cabinet with plastic ties. Ensure nothing gets between the fan blades. Do not leave behind screws or other metallic objects inside the case.

- **Setup the BIOS**: Refer to the motherboard manual and setup the BIOS. Most importantly, select the DVD or USB drive that will function as the temporary boot drive so that you can install the OS.

- **Install OS and drivers**: Switch on computer and install the OS on a partition on the HDD. In Windows, you will have to first install the chipset drivers first and restart the computer. You can install other drivers for onboard devices from the motherboard driver DVD. Connect a LAN cable to the ethernet port of the motherboard. An LED in the port should start blinking if a proper connection is made. Configure networking and download driver updates. You can install x1 PCIe add-on devices at a later date after the OS has been running stably for a few days. You may have to download a BIOS update and flash (install it to the motherboard BIOS memory). This will most likely solve any lingering hardware problems. The motherboard manual or the website will tell you how to update the BIOS. Store driver CDs and manuals in a safe place.

Well, you have finished the book. If you give it a good rating (☆ ☆ ☆ ☆ ☆) or review online, it would be much appreciated. If you have any corrections or suggestions, write to me at Info@VSubhash.Com.

Annexure 1: PC History

The CPU of today has evolved quite a bit from what was known as the *microprocessor*. The first microprocessor was initially designed by a Japanese company named Busicom who needed it for a programmable calculator. They asked Intel to develop it further and the *4004* microprocessor was the result. It was released in 1971 and that was the first time that several parts that used to be separate in older computer designs came together as one computing unit.

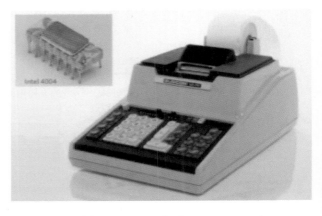

The Intel microprocessor underwent several generations of development and achieved considerable market success. In 1973, Xerox Corporation had something called a "personal workstation." It was a research project limited to Xerox installations and a few universities. It could not be used at home.

Xerox PARC history

So, the job of inventing the personal computer was left to a guy named Gary Kildall. Not even Intel knew their processors could be used on a desktop. If you check the archives of the American TV program 'Computer Chronicles', you will find an episode titled 'Gary Kildall Special' that will make it clear as to who invented the PC.

> ... Killdall had started developing his Control Program for Microcomputers (CP/M) in the early 1970s when he realized the potential for a general-purpose small computer. He was carrying a

portable computer at a time when a desktop PC was just a dream.

Tom Rolander (first DRI employee): "I met Gary in 1973 in the Computer Science Lab late one evening. He was a young kid ... He came into the computer center with a leather briefcase that he flipped open that he connected to a teletype ... and that was an entire self-contained computer. It was the first personal computer I ever saw."

... Gordon Eubanks (another DRI employee, later Norton AV, later Symantec): "... he invented a programming language called PL/M and implemented it for the Intel microprocessors to prove that that 8080 was a real computer and not a controller for microwave ovens ...

... while a consultant at Intel in the 70s, he offered to sell them CP/M but Intel could see no use for it and turned him down. Shortly afterwards in 1976, Gary and his wife Dorothy founded a company called InterGalactic Digital Research, later shortened to Digital Research ...

Gary's design allowed programs written for CP/M to be used on hardware produced by different manufacturers. Thus, CP/M started a whole new industry for personal computing.

In 1977, Steve Jobs started marketing a "personal computer" designed by Steve Wozniak. Their Apple II personal computer was targeted at the masses, unlike CP/M-loaded PC kits targeted at hobbyists and engineers. Apple II was one of several commercially successful personal computers. When Steve Jobs kicked the bucket, several morons (including one US president) claimed that Jobs invented the personal computer, the mouse, the smartphone, the wheel, fire, the lightbulb, sliced bread, music, media players and indoor plumbing.

In the early 1980s, IBM chose Intel's 8086 microprocessor as the CPU for the first *IBM Personal Computer*. As part of the agreement with IBM, Intel was asked to license the technology to a second supplier so that IBM did not have suffer any supply disruption from one of them. The second supplier that Intel chose was a startup named AMD (American Micro Devices). Intel's fortunes received a massive boost when the IBM PC became a phenomenal success. However, IBM lost control of the market to makers of IBM PC clones. Intel then felt it was not tied to IBM contracts anymore and unsuccessfully tried to stop AMD from making Intel-compatible CPUs. Meanwhile, Cyrix and NEC copied Intel processors' computing instructions set and built an Intel-compatible chip. Cyrix was eventually bought by Via Technologies, which has almost no presence in the market now.

- **Undead Myths In The Wake Of iDead Steve Jobs**
  http://www.vsubhash.in/undead-myths-in-the-wake-of-idead-steve-jobs.html
  - **Xerox PARC History**
    https://www.parc.com/about-parc/parc-history/
- **Intel 4004**
  https://www.intel.com/content/www/us/en/newsroom/resources/intel-4004.html

Books By V. Subhash

I invite you to visit my site **WWW.VSUBHASH.IN**, and check out my other books, special discounts, sample PDFs and full ebooks. In 2020, I started publishing books. For two decades before that, I have been publishing feature articles, free ebooks (old editions still available), software (server/desktop/mobile), reviews (books, films, music and travel), funny memes and cartoons. You can follow these adventures on my blog: **http://www.vsubhash.in/blogs/blog/index.html**

My books for children are under the pseudonym **Ólafía L. Óla** (because it has laugh and LOL).

 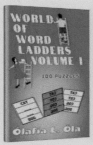 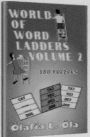 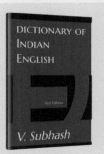

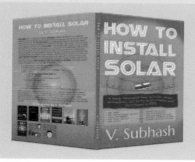

About the author

V. **Subhash** is an invisible Indian writer, programmer and cartoonist. In 2020, he published one of the biggest jokebooks of all time and then followed it up with a tech book on FFmpeg and a 400-page volume of 149 political cartoons. Although he had published a few ebooks as early as 2003, Subhash did not publish books in the traditional sense until 2020. For over two decades, Subhash had used his website **www.VSubhash.com** as the main outlet for his writing. During this time, he had accumulated a lot of published and unpublished material. This content and the automated book-production process that he had developed helped him publish 21 books in his first year. In February 2023, Apress (SpringerNature) published his rewritten and updated FFmpeg book as *QUICK START GUIDE TO FFMPEG*. Thus, by early 2023, Subhash had published 30 books! In 2022, Subhash ran out of non-fiction material and tried his hand at fiction. The result was *UNLIKELY STORIES*, a collection of horror and comedy short stories. After adding new stories to this fiction title (for its second edition), Subhash plans to pause his writing and move on to other things. Subhash pursues numerous hobbies and interests, several of which have become the subject of his books such as *COOL ELECTRONIC PROJECTS*, *HOW TO INSTALL SOLAR* and *HOW TO INVEST IN STOCKS*. He was inspired to write his jokebook after years of listening to vintage American radio shows such as *Fibber & Molly* and *Duffy's Tavern*.